SHARK-TASTIC

BY LORI STEIN

downtown bookworks

downtown 🏢 bookworks

Shark Consultant: Yannis Papastamatiou

Designed by Georgia Rucker

Typeset in Bryant Pro and Warugaki

PHOTO CREDITS 1–3: Shutterstock.com (all). 4: ©Alberto Pomares/iStockphoto.com. 4–5: ©Minden Pictures/SuperStock. 6: Shutterstock.com (all). 7: ©Sergey Kashkin/iStockphoto.com (TL), ©emmgunn/ iStockphoto.com (TR), ©Tan Klan Khoon/iStockphoto.com (CR), ©Paulbanton72/Dreamstime.com (B). 8: Shutterstock.com. 8–9: Shutterstock.com. 9: ©Minden Pictures/SuperStock.com. 10–11: ©Willtu/ Dreamstime.com. 11: ©Photomyeye/Dreamstime.com. 12: ©Doug Perrine/SeaPics.com. 13: ©Can Stock Photo Inc., 2011 (T), ©Howard Hall/SeaPics.com (B). 14: ©Jeff Rotman/SeaPics.com (T), ©Chrismoncrieff/ Dreamstime.com (B). 14–15: ©Crisod/Dreamstime.com. 15: ©Krzysztof Odziomek/iStockphoto.com. 16: ©Thediver123/Dreamstime.com. 16–17: ©Andy Murch/SeaPics.com. 17: ©Visual & Written/SuperStock. 18: ©Amanda Cotton/iStockphoto.com (T). Shutterstock.com (B). 19: Courtesy Matthew Field/GNU Free Documentation License (T), ©Minden Pictures/SuperStock (C), Shutterstock.com (B). 20: ©Mark Conlin VWPics/SuperStock. 20–21: Shutterstock.com. 21: ©Ian Scott/iStockphoto.com (T), Shutterstock.com (B). 22: ©David Shen/SeaPics.com (TL), ©Marty Snyderman/SeaPics.com (TR), Courtesy Avenue/GNU Free Documentation License (BL), ©Gwen Lowe/SeaPics.com (BR). 23: ©Teguhtirta/Dreamstime.com (T), Gregory B. Skomal/SWFSC-NOAA (B). 24: Shutterstock.com (all). 25: ©C & M Fallows/SeaPics.com (T), ©Doug Perrine/SeaPics.com (B). 26: ©Thediver123/Dreamstime.com (T), Shutterstock.com (L). 27: Shutterstock.com (T), ©Dynamail/Dreamstime.com (B). 28: Shutterstock.com (TR, TCL, B), ©VMJones/ iStockphoto.com (TL), ©Birgul Ozbek Erken (BCL). 29: ©Pacific Stock/SuperStock (TL), ©George W. Benz/ SeaPics.com (CR), ©George Schellenger/iStockphoto.com (BL). 30: ©C & M Fallows/Oceanwideimages.com. 31: Shutterstock.com (all). 32: ©Chris Huss/SeaPics.com. 33: Courtesy Citron/CC-BY-SA-3.0/GNU Free Documentation License (TR), public domain (BL). 34: ©Cor Bosman/iStockphoto.com (TL), Shutterstock.com (BL), ©William Davies/iStockphoto.com (BR). 35: ©Nathanc78/Dreamstime.com (TR), ©Uxpix1/Dreamstime.com (CR). 36–37: © Naluphoto/Dreamstime.com. 37: Shutterstock.com. 38: Shutterstock.com. 39: ©Ligio/Dreamstime.com (T), ©Island Effects/iStockphoto.com (B). 40: ©Thediver123/ Dreamstime.com (T), Shutterstock.com (B). 41: ©Gnohz/Dreamstime.com (TR), ©Andidream/Dreamstime.com (B). 42–45: Shutterstock.com (all). 46: ©Plasmatic/Dreamstime.com (border), ©Tektite/Dreamstime.com (teeth). 47: ©IndexStock/SuperStock (TR), ©AnnaOmelchenko/Dreamstime.com (BL). 48: ©Jacquesklopper/ Dreamstime.com (background), ©Rookiedi/Dreamstime.com (TR), ©Pat Bonish/iStockphoto.com (TL).

Printed in China, May 2011

ISBN 9781935703297

10 9 8 7 6 5 4 3 2 1

Downtown Bookworks Inc.
285 West Broadway
New York, NY 10013
www.downtownbookworks.com

CONTENTS

KINGS OF THE OCEAN

There are about 400 different kinds of sharks, and they are found in every ocean on Earth. They range from tiny (about eight inches) to huge (more than 40 feet long). Some are fast and aggressive; some are slow and gentle.

Sharks are excellent swimmers. In fact, some sharks are the fastest fish alive. Scientists and inventors designed submarines, torpedoes, and yachts to have shapes similar to shark bodies.

Mako shark

New kinds of sharks are found all the time. One of the coolest ones is the megamouth shark, which has a gigantic, toothy mouth. It was discovered after it got caught in the anchor of a Navy ship in 1976.

Because sharks eat so many different kinds of animals, they can have a big impact on the populations of ocean wildlife.

Some sharks are both coordinated and extremely fast, which helps to make them the ocean's top predators.

5

THE WIDE WORLD OF SHARKS

Sharks come in many different shapes, sizes, and colors. Check them out!

The **oceanic white tip shark** is very aggressive. This shark has been known to attack shipwrecked sailors.

Their yellow color gives **lemon sharks** their name. Very common in the Gulf of Mexico, they can blend in with the sandy bottom of shallow water.

The **nurse shark** hangs out on the ocean floor and waits for for food to come near it.

Bull sharks are big eaters. They eat large fish, dolphins, other sharks, and even humans. They are happy in freshwater, and can sometimes be found in rivers.

The **leopard shark's** spots help to camouflage this small shark on the ocean floor, so bigger predators have a hard time spotting it.

Sand tiger sharks look scary, but they won't bother you unless you bother them first. They usually stay on the sandy ocean bottom.

Hammerhead sharks are known for the interesting shape of their heads.

The **great white** is the scariest shark because it's most likely to attack humans.

THE BODY OF THE BEAST

Sharks are not all the same, but there are some features that most sharks have in common.

Eyes Shark eyes are on the sides of their heads, which lets them see prey over a wide patch of ocean.

Snouts and nostrils Sharks don't use their nostrils to breathe—they use them only for smelling.

Pectoral fin

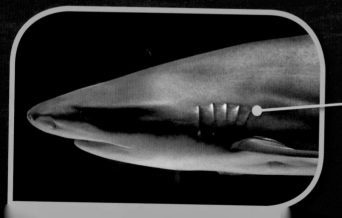

Gills Sharks breathe through their gills. Most fish have only one set of gills, but sharks have five, six, or seven sets. This allows them to take in a lot of oxygen so they can keep

Dorsal fin This is the fin on top of a shark's body. You may see one sticking out of the water when a shark is near.

Fins Most sharks have five types of fins. Sharks use their fins to swim and to keep balanced in the water.

In the past, people used sharkskin as sandpaper.

Skin Sharks have rough skin made up of tiny pieces called denticles.

Pectoral fin

Tail fin

Pelvic fin

Anal fin

Sharks move forward by using their tails as propellers. They can swim hundreds of miles a day.

9

SCARIEST
FISH ALIVE

Great whites are only half white—the bottom half. On top, they're gray, so that they blend in with the ocean floor.

Great white sharks are responsible for about half of the shark attacks on humans. Their favorite foods are sea lions, seals, and small whales, but they'll eat many kinds of fish. They don't particularly like humans because we're too bony. Sometimes, after taking a bite of a human, a great white will let go and look for something tastier. An average of 15 feet long, great whites can weigh more than 5,000 pounds.

Great white

Great whites have an awesome sense of smell. They are great at detecting certain chemicals found in the blood of their prey. They may even pick up on blood that is several miles away!

Great whites are among the few sharks that will jump right out of the water when chasing prey.

Great whites can swim up to 15 miles per hour.

WHERE DO SHARK BABIES COME FROM?

A lemon shark gives birth to live pups in a shallow lagoon.

Shark babies are called pups. Different sharks give birth in different ways. Most sharks—like hammerheads, bull sharks, and lemon sharks—give birth to live babies. Their pregnancies can last from six months to two years. Like humans, these babies get food from their mothers in the womb.

There are other sharks that carry eggs inside their bodies but do not nourish the embryos during pregnancy. (Embryos are what the growing shark babies are called before they are born.) Instead, these embryos eat the unfertilized eggs and other embryos around them. Sand tiger sharks develop this way. They come out fighting, eating their brothers and sisters.

Some sharks—like the zebra shark, swell shark, and horn shark—lay eggs. These eggs have a yolk (like a chicken egg) that feeds the embryo. Shark eggs are laid in little cases called mermaid's purses. Shark moms drop these egg cases on the ocean floor, usually in pairs, and it takes nine to 12 months for them to hatch.

Egg-laying sharks do not guard their eggs. Most mother sharks don't care for their pups once they're born, either. The mother shark takes her pups to a safe place and abandons them. Luckily, the pups are born with a full set of teeth, so they can protect themselves.

Look closely at this mermaid's purse and you can see the baby shark forming inside.

A baby horn shark hatches from its spiral-shaped egg case.

MINI AND MASSIVE

We think of sharks as huge, and some of them are. But there are also sharks that are small enough to fit in your hands.

Spined pygmy shark

The smallest sharks—lantern sharks, cat sharks, dogfish sharks, and pygmy sharks—are less than 10 inches long. One of the tiniest is the pale cat shark, which is only 8 1/4 inches long. That's only two inches longer than a dollar bill.

Cat shark

The biggest sharks—and the biggest fish alive—are **whale sharks**. They are gentle giants with tiny teeth. Whale sharks swim slowly through the deep ocean and eat only small fish that accidentally swim into their huge mouths.

Whale sharks are more than 40 feet long, about the size of a bus.

These calm creatures almost never attack humans.

CATS AND DOGS

There are about 150 species of little sharks called cat sharks. They are pretty small—most are less than two feet long—and they have slanty eyes like cats. Some, like tiger cat sharks and pajama cat sharks, have stripes, while others—like the yellow-spotted cat shark and the leopard cat shark—have spots.

One type of cat shark has a funny name: the dogfish shark. Dogfish sharks got their name because they hunt for food in packs. There are sometimes more than 1,000 dogfish sharks in a pack.

Spiny dogfish are among the most common sharks in the world.

The beautiful **chain cat shark** has bright green eyes and markings all over its body that look like they were painted on.

Swell sharks are a really cool group of cat sharks. Also known as balloon sharks, they have a clever way to get predators to leave them alone. When a swell shark is frightened by another fish, it swallows a lot of water or air so its body balloons to about three times its normal size. This scares off bigger predators.

California swell shark

TIGERS AND LEOPARDS

Tiger sharks live up to their name. They are ferocious predators that attack sea turtles, sea birds, squids, and sometimes humans. Tiger sharks are called "garbage guts." They eat everything, including tin cans, tires, and handbags. Leopard sharks are more like pussycats; other sharks eat them all the time, and there's no record of a leopard shark ever biting a human being.

In 2003, a 15-foot tiger shark attacked teenage surfer Bethany Hamilton and bit off her arm. With help from a friend, she got to shore and survived the attack. She recovered, and taught herself to surf competitively with one arm.

Tiger sharks get their name from the patterns on their skin when they are young. As tiger sharks get older, their stripes fade away.

Leopard shark

Leopard sharks are social animals. They form schools with other leopard sharks, and hang around with dogfish sharks and gray sharks.

Tiger sharks are solitary animals. They travel and hunt by themselves.

HAMMERHEADS

There are nine kinds of hammerhead sharks. The biggest is the great hammerhead, which can grow up to 20 feet long and weigh up to 1,000 pounds. Great hammerheads don't eat humans, but try not to bump into one—they're so big that you're bound to get hurt.

Great hammerhead

The head of a hammerhead shark is the perfect shape to pin stingrays to the ocean floor so the sharks can kill and eat them.

The hammerhead's eyes are spaced far apart, which helps it track its prey over a wide area. Hammerheads are especially sensitive to electrical impulses sent out by other fish.

Hammerheads are among the few large sharks that swim in schools. They seem to get along with each other.

Scalloped hammerheads have very large brains, and some scientists think they are especially smart.

WEIRD SHARKS

Here are some of the oddest-looking sharks around.

Goblin sharks are very rare. They have dragon-like horns on their heads.

Saw sharks look like they swallowed a tool from a carpenter's workbench. They use their long, toothy snout to cut up prey until it is small enough to eat.

Sometimes, fishermen catch big fish with odd, round wounds on their bodies. That means that the cookie-cutter shark is in town. These small sharks have round mouths with very sharp teeth and take bites from bigger fish. They're not deadly, just very annoying.

Cookie-cutter shark

Wobbegong sharks are flat, puffy fish that look a little like old-fashioned rugs; they are part of a group known as carpet sharks. They don't get around much. Mostly, they lie on the ocean floor waiting to snap up small fish, octopuses, and crabs, with their razor-sharp teeth. Wobbegongs are excellent at camouflage: they blend right in to the ocean floor.

Basking sharks swim with their huge mouths wide open. Each has about 1,000 tiny rakes in its mouth and can filter up to 2,000 tons of water every hour. As they swim, small fish and plankton stick to the rakes. When a shark has a mouthful of fish, it closes its mouth and swallows.

23

EXTREME SHARKS

Whale shark

Biggest mouth
The mouth of a whale shark can be four and a half feet wide.

Longest
The whale shark is the longest fish in the world. It often grows to be 40 feet long. One whale shark caught near Thailand in 1919 was more than 59 feet long.

Longest-distance swimmers
Blue sharks have been tracked as they migrate from New York to Brazil. That's more than 4,000 miles! Scientists use electronic tags to get information about the sharks' travel routes.

Most babies
Whale sharks can lay up to 300 eggs, and blue sharks can deliver up to 135 pups at a time.

Blue shark

Fastest

Shortfin mako sharks are the fastest. One was clocked at 68 miles per hour, but only for a short burst.

Strongest bite

Dusky sharks bite with more force than all other sharks, about 132 pounds per inch. Ouch!

Dusky shark

Thresher shark

Longest tail

The thresher shark's tail can grow to be 10 feet long, which is as long as the rest of its body. Threshers use their tails to stun prey.

SHARK SENSE

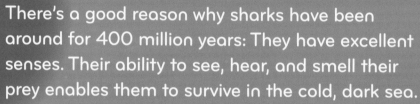

There's a good reason why sharks have been around for 400 million years: They have excellent senses. Their ability to see, hear, and smell their prey enables them to survive in the cold, dark sea.

Sharks smell through their nostrils, which are on their snouts. When they swim, water passes through their nostrils. Tiny parts of all kinds of smelly things—fish and blood in particular—stimulate receptors in their nostrils, and sharks know what is in the area. The amazing part is that they can "sense" a smell when there's only a tiny bit of it. Their sense of smell is much better than ours.

Sharks don't hear the way we do. They don't have ears outside their heads, but they're not deaf. Sharks' ears are inside their skulls. They are like little tunnels filled with fluid. Sound waves bounce around in this fluid, and the shark senses that something is making a noise.

Sharks have an extra sense that turns them into superfish. It is called electroreception. When other fish move in the ocean, they give off tiny electrical currents. Sharks have receptors on their snouts that let them feel these currents, so they know just where the prey is.

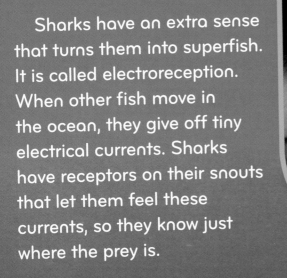

The receptors that let sharks sense the presence of other fish are called **ampullae of Lorenzini**. They look like a rash.

As sharks swim through the ocean, they use their senses of sight, hearing, smell, and electroreception to find food.

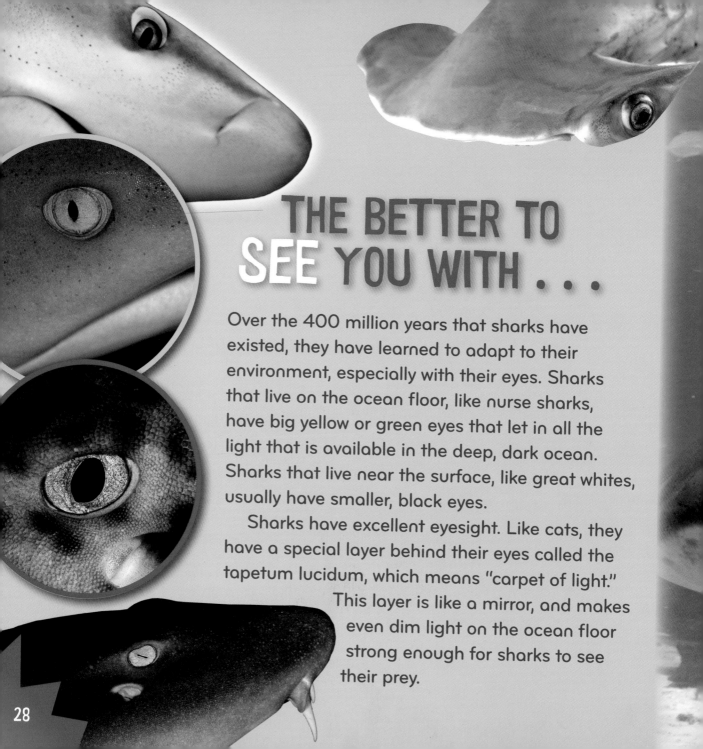

THE BETTER TO SEE YOU WITH . . .

Over the 400 million years that sharks have existed, they have learned to adapt to their environment, especially with their eyes. Sharks that live on the ocean floor, like nurse sharks, have big yellow or green eyes that let in all the light that is available in the deep, dark ocean. Sharks that live near the surface, like great whites, usually have smaller, black eyes.

Sharks have excellent eyesight. Like cats, they have a special layer behind their eyes called the tapetum lucidum, which means "carpet of light." This layer is like a mirror, and makes even dim light on the ocean floor strong enough for sharks to see their prey.

Some sharks have a membrane over their eyes that protects their eyeballs while they are ripping apart their prey. Sharks that don't have this membrane, like great whites, roll their eyes back during a feeding frenzy.

Tiger shark

Greenland sharks are often blind. Wormy parasites attach to their eyes and feed on them.

LUNCH

Great white sharks eat up to 11 tons of food a year.

Almost all sharks are carnivores. That means that they eat meat, not plants. Some sharks, like bull sharks and tiger sharks, eat the biggest animals they can find, like seals, turtles, whales, even other sharks. Then there are sharks, including big ones such as whale sharks and basking sharks, that eat tiny organisms, like plankton, clams, and very small fish.

enormous mouth, it eats only small fish and tiny organisms.

After a shark eats a big meal, it will sometimes not eat at all for days or even months. That's because it stores food, in the form of oil, in its large liver.

Sharks have awesome talents and abilities when it comes to eating. In addition to smelling food, they can also hear it. There's something called a yummy hum—a low-frequency sound that weakened fish send out. Sharks can track and catch prey easily because they are fast swimmers. And they have strong jaws and teeth, so they can rip apart their prey after they catch them.

Lemon sharks eat many animals, including stingrays, sea birds, squid, crabs, and other sharks.

Some sharks will eat anything, including garbage. Some of the things found in sharks' stomachs are shoes, gas tanks, clothing, and license plates.

ANCIENT SHARKS

There were sharks in the oceans about 400 million years ago—long before there were dinosaurs on Earth. Although dinosaurs disappeared, sharks evolved. Over millions of years, they gained new senses and body parts to help them survive. The earliest sharks did not have all the fins that allow modern sharks to stay balanced. Today's shark is a great example of evolution.

Scientists have started a project to measure how long sharks live. They catch baby sharks, put electronic bands on them, and then release them. When the sharks stop breathing, the bands transmit a signal to the scientists to let them know that the shark is dead.

Though we know that sharks have been around for a *really* long time, it's hard to know which shark lives the longest. Some scientists say that **spiny dogfish sharks** have the longest lives, up to 60 years. Others say that whale sharks can live 100 years.

The **frilled shark** is also called a fossil shark. This type of shark has been around for millions of years. Most of the sharks that we see today are descendants of these ancient types.

This is a model of the jaws of the monster **Megalodon**. The animal's jaws could be 10 feet wide!

One of the most frightening creatures that ever lived was the Megalodon, a shark that lived more than a million years ago. Megalodons grew up to 60 feet long, and had six-inch teeth. Megalodons bit with so much force, they could crush a T. rex to bits in just seconds.

SHARK ATTACK

Sharks do attack humans, but not very often. Each year there are 50 to 70 reports from all over the world of sharks biting humans. You have more chance of being killed by a bee sting or by a coconut falling from a tree than by a shark attack.

Four sharks are responsible for almost all shark attacks. Great whites are by far the most likely to attack a person, followed by tiger sharks, bull sharks, and oceanic white tips. A few other sharks, including hammerheads, makos, silky, blue, and lemon sharks,

Tiger shark

WARNING

6

Sharks may be present
Shark bites have occurred in this area

Great white shark

have attacked humans a couple of times each in all of recorded history.

Until the 20th century, people didn't worry much about sharks. Then, in 1916, four swimmers were killed by sharks near beaches in New Jersey, and people started worrying about sharks.

In 1945, after delivering the atomic bomb to the Air Force, the naval ship U.S.S. *Indianapolis* was torpedoed, and 900 men went into the Pacific Ocean. The next morning, sharks started circling. Four days later, rescuers picked up about 300 survivors; many of the rest had been killed by sharks.

After the *Indianapolis* disaster, the Navy started searching for shark repellents. They found that copper, soap, and electrical shocks drive sharks away.

Bull shark

Oceanic white tip shark

About 15 people are killed by sharks each year. People kill millions of sharks each year.

HOW DO SHARKS PASS THE TIME?

If you're a shark, you don't have a lot of activities planned on most days. Your main activity is breathing. Sharks don't breathe through their nostrils. Instead, many use a process called ram ventilation. They take water into their mouths and swim forward, pushing the water through their gills to get the oxygen out of it. That is why many sharks need to keep moving, or they will drown.

Most sharks also have strong muscles that let them process the water in their gills even when they're not moving. This process is called buccal breathing. Those sharks, such as nurse sharks and spiny dogfish sharks, can take pretty long rest periods. Angel sharks can stay still for up to two days.

Tiger sharks often spend their days in deeper waters, then move closer to the surface at night to hunt.

Most sharks don't hang around with other sharks, though there are exceptions such as hammerheads and dogfish sharks, which like to travel in schools and packs. But even loner sharks sometimes join parties called feeding frenzies. When sharks see another shark eating, they often rush toward the meal. All the sharks go a little crazy, grabbing at the food. Feeding frenzies can be very intense!

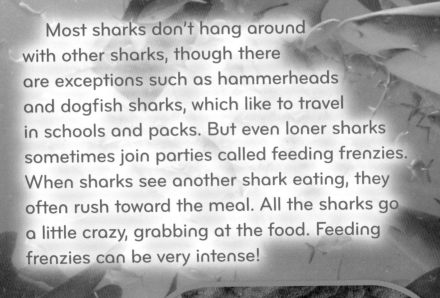

Angel sharks look for food at night. During the day, they bury themselves in the mud or sand. When certain types of fish come close, the angel shark ambushes its prey!

SWIMMING WITH SHARKS

Sharks are very rarely alone. A few types of small fish hang around with sharks—even with the biggest and baddest ones. They have what's called symbiotic (sim-bye-ah-tik) relationships: Both the sharks and their small friends benefit from being together.

Pilot fish

One fish that follows sharks around is the pilot fish. Pilot fish eat parasites—wormy little things—off the sharks. And the sharks protect the pilot fish from bigger fish. Sometimes a pilot fish will swim right into a shark's mouth and eat crud off its teeth.

Remora

Remora literally stick to sharks. These small, grayish-brown fish have little suckers that allow them to attach themselves to the sides of sharks. Remora also clean dirt and parasites from the sharks. The remora get to hitch rides and avoid swimming all day long, and the sharks get a grooming service.

SHARKS AND US

People have used sharks for centuries. Shark oil is full of vitamins, omega-3 fatty acids, and other nutrients.Fishermen and lots of other people use it to keep healthy.

Shark leather is very thick and strong; boots made of shark leather will last for many years. And before sandpaper was invented, people rubbed sharkskin on rough surfaces to smooth them down. Some people also eat shark meat.

In the future, sharks may be even more helpful to humans. Sharks almost never get sick, and very rarely get cancer. Scientists are trying to figure out what makes them so healthy. Some believe that learning more about sharks may help researchers find a cure for cancer.

Sometimes, humans treat sharks terribly. Some fishermen catch sharks and cut off their fins to use for shark-fin soup, which is considered a special meal in China. The fishermen then throw the sharks back. Sharks can't swim without fins, and they drown. Millions of sharks are killed this way each year. Many people are trying to stop this cruel practice. Shark-fin soup is banned in some places, including Oregon, Hawaii, and Honduras.

Shark-fin soup

Shark fins

TWIST AND TURN

Sharks have no bones. The only hard things in their bodies are their jaws and teeth. Instead of bones, they have cartilage, a firm but flexible tissue. If you want to know what cartilage feels like, grab the tip of your nose or the top of your ear and jiggle it. The stuff that keeps our ears and noses stiff but movable is cartilage, and that's what keeps a shark's body from caving in.

Having cartilage instead of bones makes a shark's body flexible and able to twist and turn. They can bend their bodies to reach into corners to catch their prey—and then use their sharp, solid teeth to bite and tear into it.

STRANGE BUT TRUE

Sharks can only swim forward.

A shark eats a lot of bony, crusty things. When it can't digest something, it vomits out its whole stomach and lets the indigestible things fall out. It then swallows its stomach, returning it to its rightful place.

When a male shark wants to let a female shark know that he is interested in mating, he bites her, hard, on her body or fins.

About 90% of shark attacks have been on men, even though women spend just as much time in the ocean.

Most sharks are only found in salt water, but bull sharks can live in freshwater as well. To do so, they drink a lot of water and then urinate about 20 times as much as usual, so that the salt level inside their bodies adjusts to the salt level outside of them.

Most sharks are silent; they do not have voice boxes. But there is a swell shark in New Zealand that barks like a dog.

THAT BITES!

Sharks don't need dentists for their super-sharp teeth. Their mouths are filled with rows and rows of teeth.
When a tooth breaks or becomes loose, it falls out, and a tooth from the row behind it moves up. It takes only a few days for the new tooth to be ready to rip into prey.

Sharks can go through 20,000 teeth in a lifetime. That's why it's easy to find old shark teeth on the beach.

Sharks don't chew. They use their teeth to tear their food into pieces small enough to swallow.

Sharks lose teeth every time they eat.

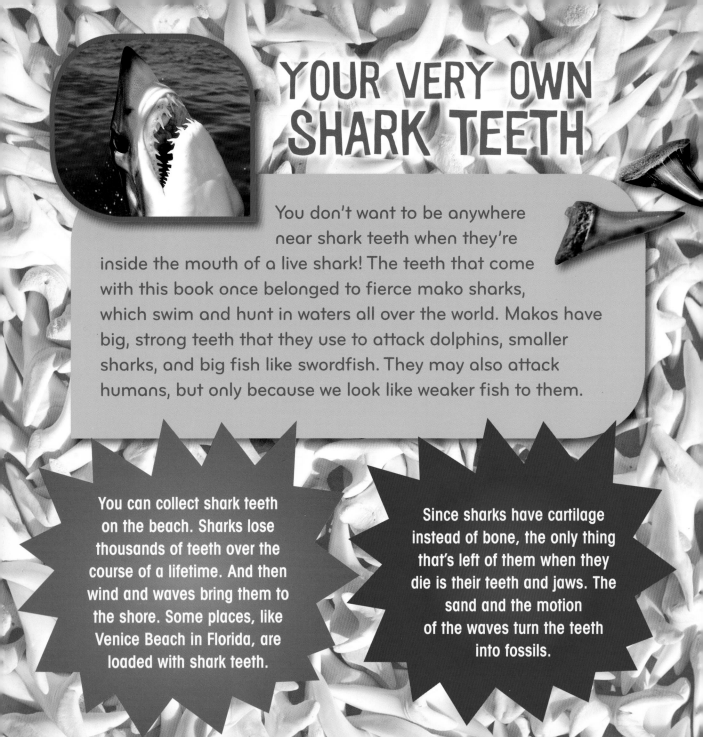

YOUR VERY OWN SHARK TEETH

You don't want to be anywhere near shark teeth when they're inside the mouth of a live shark! The teeth that come with this book once belonged to fierce mako sharks, which swim and hunt in waters all over the world. Makos have big, strong teeth that they use to attack dolphins, smaller sharks, and big fish like swordfish. They may also attack humans, but only because we look like weaker fish to them.

You can collect shark teeth on the beach. Sharks lose thousands of teeth over the course of a lifetime. And then wind and waves bring them to the shore. Some places, like Venice Beach in Florida, are loaded with shark teeth.

Since sharks have cartilage instead of bone, the only thing that's left of them when they die is their teeth and jaws. The sand and the motion of the waves turn the teeth into fossils.